Original title:
Love What You Do

Author: Clement Portlander
ISBN HARDBACK: 978-9916-88-034-0
ISBN PAPERBACK: 978-9916-88-035-7

The Spirit of the Artisan

In every hand, a story weaves,
Crafted dreams that time believes.
The sculptor bends the silent stone,
With chisel's kiss, each form is grown.

Upon the loom, the weaver sighs,
Colors dance, 'neath watchful eyes.
Each thread a tale, each knot a bond,
In fabric's embrace, we respond.

The painter strokes a vibrant hue,
Upon the canvas ideals anew.
Brushes dance in swirling flight,
Capturing shadows, day, and night.

In every craft, a heartbeat beats,
Passion flows where labor meets.
With spirit bright, the artisan stands,
Creating beauty with skilled hands.

The Symphony of Engagement

In every sound our voices meet,
A harmony we can't defeat.
With hearts as one, we sing as true,
Creating magic, me and you.

Moments shared in laughter bright,
Together we'll soar to new height.
Each note a promise, softly played,
In this symphony, we won't fade.

Fueling the Soul

In whispers soft, the fire glows,
With every breath, our passion grows.
The warmth ignites, a dance anew,
Fueling dreams and visions true.

With every step, our spirits rise,
Chasing stars in velvet skies.
The flame within, it lights the way,
Fueling hope for each new day.

Resonance of Resolve

With steadfast hearts, we pave the road,
In unity, we share the load.
A beacon shines through darkest night,
In every struggle, we find light.

Together strong, we stand our ground,
In every setback, we are bound.
The echoes of our voices blend,
In resolve, our spirits mend.

The Art of Heartfelt Endeavors

In every gesture, love displayed,
A masterpiece that won't degrade.
With open arms, we craft our fate,
The art of kindness can't wait.

In shared endeavors, hope awakes,
With every heartbeat, a chance it takes.
Through trials faced, we find our way,
A vibrant canvas, day by day.

Whispers of Dedication

In quiet moments, we find our way,
With whispers soft, we choose to stay.
The heartbeats echo, strong and true,
In every promise, I cherish you.

Through trials faced, we stand as one,
In shadows deep, our light has won.
With every whisper, love's embrace,
We tread together, time can't erase.

The Dance of Devotion

In the twilight glow, our shadows sway,
With grace and warmth, we find our play.
Each step we take, in rhythm's flow,
A sacred bond, forever grows.

Around us, stars align above,
In every twirl, we weave our love.
With laughter bright, and hearts that sing,
In this sweet dance, our souls take wing.

In Pursuit of Joy

With open hearts, we chase the sun,
Through fields of dreams, we always run.
In laughter shared, we find our grace,
In every moment, a warm embrace.

The world is vast, but hand in hand,
Together, we explore and stand.
In every heartbeat, joy we find,
A treasure rare, so sweet, so kind.

Emblems of Enthusiasm

With fiery spirits, we rise each day,
Our voices strong, we find our way.
In every dream, ambition shines,
A testament, our hope aligns.

With open minds, we greet the dawn,
In every challenge, we carry on.
Emblems bright of passion's fire,
In every heart, our dreams inspire.

When Work Meets Heart

In quiet hours, dreams ignite,
Passion fuels the endless fight.
With every task, the spirit sings,
Love for the craft, true joy it brings.

Hands that toil, minds that strive,
In this dance, we come alive.
With heart entwined in all we do,
Success becomes a path so true.

The Alchemy of Ambition

Gold isn't found, it's forged in fire,
Dreams distill the soul's desire.
Each setback serves a greater plan,
Transforming doubt, make bold, we can.

Vision guides with steadfast light,
Every sacrifice, a step to flight.
In patience learned, we rise and shine,
The alchemy of fate divine.

Savoring the Journey

With every step, a story unfolds,
Moments cherished, memories hold.
Paths less traveled, lessons learned,
In every turn, our passions burned.

Eyes wide open, hearts embrace,
Life unwinds at its own pace.
Taste the joy, the bitter, sweet,
Each heartbeat, a rhythm, a dance, a beat.

Echoes of Purpose

Through silent whispers, we all seek,
Answers found in the words we speak.
A calling deep within our core,
Resounding truths, forevermore.

Each echo brings a guiding light,
Illuminating the paths of night.
In purpose firm, we stand and rise,
With open hearts, we reach the skies.

Elysium of Enthusiasm

In fields of dreams where passions soar,
Each heartbeat whispers, 'Seek for more.'
With every step, we chase the light,
Together we stand, ready to ignite.

Amidst the clouds where visions play,
We carve our paths, come what may.
With fire in our souls, we rise,
In Elysium, our spirits prize.

Symphony of Dedication

In harmony, our voices blend,
With every note, we rise and mend.
Through trials faced, our spirits strong,
In the symphony, we all belong.

With heartbeats echoing, dreams take flight,
In dedication, we find our might.
The rhythm guides us, hand in hand,
Together we stand, a united band.

Crafting Futures with Heart

Through hands that mold and dreams that guide,
We build the world with love inside.
Each heartbeat fuels the spark of hope,
In unity, we learn to cope.

With visions clear and passions bright,
We craft our futures, day and night.
With every choice, a story starts,
In crafting futures, we share our hearts.

The Pulse of Purpose

In rhythm found, our purpose flows,
Each heartbeat signals where we go.
With passion driving every beat,
We find our strength, we won't retreat.

In moments fleeting, we choose to stand,
With purpose clear, we join our hands.
Through challenges faced, our spirits rise,
In the pulse of purpose, our dreams comprise.

Cherished Endeavors

In the quiet moments we find our way,
Building dreams that bloom like spring,
With hearts that dance, we softly sway,
Through the challenges that life may bring.

Each effort made, a story unfolds,
With laughter shared and memories spun,
In every twist, our passion holds,
United, we rise, together as one.

Finding Bliss in the Everyday

Amidst the chaos, serenity calls,
In simple joys we find our peace,
The sunlight's glow, the soft rainfalls,
In nature's arms, troubles cease.

A steaming cup on a quiet morn,
The gentle breeze through the leaves,
Moments cherished, no need to mourn,
In every heartbeat, happiness weaves.

The Joy of Crafting Dreams

With pen in hand, we sketch our fate,
Dreams take flight on paper bright,
Each stroke defines, no need to wait,
In our imagination, day turns to night.

With vibrant colors, we paint the sky,
Creating worlds that softly gleam,
With every laugh and every sigh,
We nurture hope, we build our dream.

Crescent Moon of Ambition

Under the crescent, dreams align,
A flicker bright in the darkened night,
Each star a thought, a chance to shine,
Fueling passions with pure delight.

Though shadows linger where fears reside,
The glow within sparks the quest,
With courage held, we turn the tide,
In moonlit steps, we strive for the best.

The Art of Commitment

In shadows deep, we find our way,
With heart and will, we choose to stay.
Through trials faced, our bond will grow,
In every moment, love's vibrant glow.

Together we stand, hand in hand,
With dreams entwined, forever planned.
Through storms we weather, we rise anew,
The art of commitment, me and you.

Soulful Pursuits

In quiet whispers, dreams take flight,
We chase the stars, embracing night.
With open hearts and spirits free,
We seek the truth, our destiny.

In every rhythm, in every sound,
We dance through life, joy unbound.
With every step, our souls ignite,
In soulful pursuits, we find our light.

In the Flow of Creation

With every brush, a story told,
Colors dance, both brave and bold.
In the quiet, magic unfolds,
In the flow of creation, the heart beholds.

Ideas bloom like flowers in spring,
Inspiration comes, a gentle sting.
With every stroke, we form our fate,
In the flow of creation, we celebrate.

Vibrance in Every Stroke

A canvas waits, so bright and wide,
With dreams and hopes, we face the tide.
Each color chosen from within,
Vibrance flows, a lively spin.

Art speaks volumes, words unspoken,
In every stroke, a heart wide-open.
As beauty blooms, we're set free,
Vibrance in every stroke, pure glee.

Boundless Zeal

In the heart where dreams ignite,
Fires burn both day and night.
Chasing visions, fierce and bright,
With boundless zeal, we take to flight.

Every step, a leap of faith,
With passion, we will not hesitate.
Through the storms, we learn to thrive,
In the journey, we come alive.

Facing fears, we rise anew,
With courage as our shining hue.
In unity, our spirits soar,
With boundless zeal, we seek for more.

Colors of Creation

In a world where hues entwine,
Nature paints with strokes divine.
Every shade a story told,
In colors bright, both bold and cold.

The sun dips low, a golden sweep,
While twilight whispers secrets deep.
In the dawn, soft pastels play,
Revealing joy in a brand-new day.

From the vibrant greens of spring,
To autumn's rust, as leaves take wing.
Each moment hues will blend,
In colors of creation, we transcend.

Nurtured Talents

In gentle hands, the seeds we sow,
With tender care, we help them grow.
Nurtured dreams, we bring to light,
In the shadows, we face the night.

Each talent shines, unique and rare,
A symphony of strengths laid bare.
With patience stitched through every seam,
We weave the fabric of our dream.

Through trials faced, we'll find our way,
With open hearts, we'll seize the day.
In united effort, we will stand,
Nurtured talents, hand in hand.

Enchanted Endeavors

In whispered woods, where magic lies,
We seek the truth beneath the skies.
With every wish, we chase the dream,
In enchanted endeavors, we gleam.

Through hidden paths, our spirits roam,
In wonderland, we find our home.
The stars above, our guiding light,
As hearts unite and fears take flight.

With every step, the world unfolds,
In stories written, quietly bold.
With open eyes, we dare to see,
In enchanted endeavors, we are free.

Colors of Creativity

Brush of dreams in vibrant hues,
Each stroke whispers stories new.
Imagination takes to flight,
In the canvas of the night.

Dancing shades that boldly play,
In the heart where muses stay.
Creating worlds with every glance,
In the art of pure romance.

Sparks of joy in every shade,
In the colors, spirits wade.
Let the palette guide your soul,
In this vibrant, wondrous stroll.

With each hue, a tale to tell,
Dare to weave your magic well.
For in colors, life we find,
A symphony of heart and mind.

Flourish in Your Calling

In the silence, hear your song,
A whisper where you belong.
Through the trials, let hope rise,
Follow dreams that light the skies.

Nurture seeds of thought and deed,
From your heart, let passion lead.
With each step, just feel the flow,
In the journey, love will grow.

Hands outstretched to grasp the day,
In the sun, let worries sway.
Blooming bright, your spirit free,
Flourish in your destiny.

Cherish moments, small and grand,
Find the rhythm, understand.
In your calling, let love soar,
Embrace the life you long for.

The Beauty of Pursuit

Chasing dreams like stars at night,
In the shadows, find your light.
Every step a chance to grow,
In the struggle, beauty flows.

Paths unknown and trails to blaze,
In the journey, hearts ablaze.
With each turn, a lesson learned,
In the fire, our passion burned.

Hands that reach and hearts that yearn,
In the chase, the soul will learn.
Through the valleys, up the hills,
The beauty lies in the thrills.

Celebrate each mile you roam,
In the pursuit, you find your home.
With courage, take that daring leap,
In the chase, your dreams you'll keep.

Harvest Moon of Ambition

Underneath the harvest moon,
Dreamers gather, hearts in tune.
Nights are filled with whispered dreams,
In the glow, hope brightly beams.

Fields of gold, ambitions rise,
Reaching high towards the skies.
With each goal, a seed is sown,
In the soil, ambitions grown.

Through the toil and through the fight,
Ambition shines, a guiding light.
As the seasons come and go,
In the moon, your passions glow.

Gather strength from every phase,
Let your spirit find its ways.
In the harvest, joy you'll reap,
From the dreams that you dare keep.

Heart's True Calling

In quiet moments, truth reveals,
The echo of the heart that feels.
Through every tear and every smile,
We find our path, we walk each mile.

The gentle pull, a whispered song,
Guides us where we all belong.
In love's embrace, we find our way,
To shine our light, to be the ray.

Crafting Joy

With every brush and every hue,
We paint our dreams, we start anew.
In laughter shared, in stories told,
We weave our hearts with threads of gold.

The simple things, like morning light,
Bring warmth and spark and pure delight.
In friendship's grace, we craft our fate,
Together strong, it's never late.

Whispers of Purpose

In every shadow, there's a hint,
Of dreams and wishes, softly skint.
We search for signs, we find our way,
To follow whispers through the day.

A guiding star, so bright and near,
Calls us forward, chases fear.
With courage strong, we stand so tall,
Embracing life, we heed the call.

Dance of Devotion

With every beat, a heart in sync,
We move as one, no time to think.
In every step, a rhythm flows,
A dance of love that always grows.

Through ups and downs, we twirl and sway,
Our spirits lift, we find our way.
In sacred space, we lose our fears,
In devotion's dance, we shed our tears.

Threads of Affection

In gentle hands, we weave our care,
Stitching moments, we both share.
Each thread a promise, soft and bright,
Binding hearts in warm sunlight.

Through laughter's echo, love does grow,
In whispered secrets, soft and low.
Together we create a dance,
In every glance, a world enhanced.

Amidst the storms, we find our way,
With threads of affection, come what may.
In tapestry, our lives entwined,
A fabric rich, love redefined.

So let us thread our dreams tonight,
With every stitch, our hearts ignite.
In threads of affection, strong and true,
We sew the fabric, me and you.

Radiance in Routine

Mornings greet with sleepy eyes,
With coffee brewed, the day complies.
In simple tasks, a spark is found,
In daily rhythm, love surrounds.

From dawn to dusk, we greet the flow,
In every chore, affection grows.
Routine may seem a little plain,
Yet in its heart, joy must remain.

The little moments, side by side,
In every challenge, love is our guide.
Together we embrace the day,
Finding light in the mundane play.

So let us cherish, day by day,
The simple joy in what we say.
In routine's arms, we find our place,
A radiance in love's embrace.

Finding Bliss in Labor

With hands that toil, we ground our dreams,
In every sweat, a hope redeems.
Through labor's lens, we see the grace,
In hard work's arms, our hearts embrace.

Together we build, together we strive,
In every effort, our spirits thrive.
From dusk till dawn, we find our way,
In finding bliss in the fray.

Each challenge met, we learn and grow,
In unity's strength, the seeds we sow.
For what is labor, but love expressed,
With every task, we give our best.

So let us labor, hand in hand,
Crafting joy, close to land.
Finding bliss in all we do,
In every heartbeat, love shines through.

Caressed by Commitment

In vows we speak, our hearts unite,
In every promise, spark ignites.
Through trials faced, we stand so strong,
Caressed by commitment, where we belong.

With open arms, we share the load,
In every step, on love's road.
Through laughter's ring and tears that fall,
In commitment's cradle, we find it all.

Hold me close through storm and sun,
In every battle, we have won.
For every heartbeat, love's refrain,
Caressed by commitment, we rise again.

So let us cherish this sacred bond,
In every moment, our love responds.
In commitment's grace, we find the light,
Together forever, our hearts take flight.

Heartfelt Pursuits

In quiet moments, dreams take flight,
Whispers of hope in the soft moonlight.
Each step we take draws us near,
To treasures held ever so dear.

With every heartbeat, courage we find,
A dance of passion, body and mind.
Through trials faced, we rise and soar,
In the warmth of love, we long for more.

The journey ahead may twist and turn,
But with each lesson, we deeply learn.
Guided by heart, we will not stray,
In our heartfelt pursuits, come what may.

The Rhythm of Purpose

Each day begins with a pulse so true,
A melody guiding all that we do.
With every heartbeat, intentions align,
In the rhythm of purpose, a path we define.

Seasons may shift, and shadows may fall,
But whispers of passion beckon us all.
When challenges rise, we gather our strength,
In the dance of our dreams, we find our length.

The symphony plays, as stars softly gleam,
We follow the tunes of our deepest dream.
Bound by our vision, bold and sincere,
In the rhythm of purpose, we persevere.

Passion's Embrace

In twilight's glow, our spirits entwine,
Wrapped in the thread of a powerful sign.
With fervent gazes, we light up the dark,
In passion's embrace, igniting a spark.

Whispers of fire dance in the air,
A tapestry woven with love and care.
As we walk together, our hearts beat fast,
In the warmth of the moment, forever to last.

Each sigh a promise, each touch a song,
In the arms of desire, we surely belong.
With every heartbeat, our spirits ignite,
In passion's embrace, we find our light.

The Fire Within

Beneath the surface, a flame starts to grow,
A flicker of spirit, a radiant glow.
With each breath taken, we fan the fire,
In the depths of our souls, we fuel our desire.

Through storms and shadows, we carry the heat,
Each challenge faced makes our resolve complete.
In moments of doubt, we dig even deep,
For the fire within is ours to keep.

So let it burn brightly, let it lead the way,
Through the darkest hours, to the dawn of the day.
With passion as our compass, we will transcend,
For in the fire within, our journeys blend.

Passion's Fire

In the depths of night, we ignite,
Desires raging, burning bright.
Flickers of hope in every glance,
Together we weave a fiery dance.

A spark that leaps with every word,
In whispered dreams, our hearts are stirred.
Through tempests wild, our flames will soar,
Passion deepens, forevermore.

With eyes ablaze, we brave the storm,
In each embrace, our spirits warm.
This fire within, a guiding light,
Together we shine, fierce and right.

Let the world witness our strong desire,
For in love's embrace, we shall never tire.
With every heartbeat, our truth ignites,
Bound by passion, reaching new heights.

Heartbeats in Motion

Rhythms pulse through tender air,
Two souls dance without a care.
Every heartbeat, a shared refrain,
Together we flourish, joy and pain.

In the silence, our spirits collide,
A symphony with love as our guide.
Moments captured, forever in time,
Each heartbeat echoes, a soothing rhyme.

From dusk till dawn, we flow like rivers,
With every glance, the love shivers.
In this duet, our hearts unify,
Together we dream, soar, and fly.

In harmony, we carve our path,
With laughter and tears, we write our math.
Each heartbeat becomes our devotion,
In every pulse lies a deep emotion.

Crafting Dreams

With paintbrush strokes, we bring to life,
Imagined worlds free from strife.
Colors blend in a vivid array,
Crafting dreams that forever stay.

In whispered thoughts, ideas ignite,
Creating magic in the moonlight.
Each vision carved within the heart,
From mind to canvas, a journey starts.

Every detail holds a silent scream,
In every layer, we stitch our dream.
Through the chaos, beauty we find,
With every piece, our souls aligned.

So let your passions unfurl and soar,
Beyond the edges, seek to explore.
In crafting dreams, we find our voice,
A call to the world, a joyful choice.

Embracing the Craft

With calloused hands and weary eyes,
We build a life where passion lies.
In the heart of creation, we breathe,
Embracing the craft, our souls believe.

From wood and stone, life takes its form,
In every shape, a purpose warm.
With patience and love, we carve our fate,
In labor's toil, we celebrate.

Each rhythm, each stroke, tells a tale,
In every success and the times we fail.
Together we stand, never afraid,
Embracing the craft, our dreams are made.

With every sunset, new dawns appear,
In the warmth of our passion, we persevere.
Let's forge a legacy, sturdy and real,
In the heart of creation, our spirits heal.

Tapestry of Talents

In the loom of life we weave,
Threads of skill, we each believe.
Colors bright and textures bold,
A masterpiece we all behold.

Each talent shines, a unique light,
Guiding dreams into the night.
With every stitch, our stories sewn,
In this tapestry, we are known.

Crafted hearts and mindful hands,
In harmony, our spirit stands.
Together creating joy and pain,
A beautiful array, we gain.

With each talent, a song we sing,
A chorus of what we can bring.
In the fabric of our shared quests,
Lies the heart of our bestests.

The Heart's Canvas

Upon this canvas, emotions flow,
With every brush, true feelings show.
Colors blend, like whispers soft,
In shadows deep, the light takes off.

Each stroke reveals a hidden tale,
Of laughter, love, and times we fail.
In vibrant hues, our stories grow,
Painting dreams, where passions glow.

Boundless art in every heart,
Creating worlds, each a part.
On this canvas, hopes are laid,
In every corner, memories made.

From palette rich, to strokes divine,
A masterpiece, yours and mine.
In the colors of our days,
Art transforms in countless ways.

Passionate Footprints

Across the sands, our footprints lie,
With every step, a heartfelt sigh.
Paths we tread, stories unfold,
In the warmth, our dreams are bold.

Each mark a sign of love and grace,
Memories cherished in time and space.
Passionate trails, where we have been,
In life's journey, a shared scene.

In the soft earth, our tales are cast,
Moments linger, shadows vast.
As we wander, let hearts ignite,
In every footprint, we find light.

Together we'll trace the paths anew,
With every step, our spirits grew.
In the dance of life, we'll partake,
Each footprint speaks of the choices we make.

Unlocking Hidden Joys

In quiet corners, secrets rest,
Hidden joys, life's little quest.
With gentle hands, we seek to find,
Treasures waiting, intertwined.

Moments small, yet rich and bright,
Sparkling softly, like stars at night.
Unlocking smiles that warm the day,
In laughter's echo, worries sway.

Every glance, a chance to see,
The simple truths, where hearts agree.
In every joy, a lesson clear,
To savor life, hold love near.

With open hearts, we greet the dawn,
Unlocking bliss that lingers on.
In tiny wonders, we rejoice,
Heeding the whispers, life's true voice.

Echoes of Joyful Labor

In fields of green we toil and play,
The sun above, our guide each day.
With hands that work, spirits that soar,
Echoes of laughter, we long for more.

Each seed we plant, a hope we share,
The fruits of labor, beyond compare.
Hearts in sync, a rhythm found,
In joyful labor, love abound.

The earth responds, we feel its grace,
With every task, a warm embrace.
Together we rise, together we stand,
In echoes of joy, hand in hand.

Through sweat and toil, we grow so strong,
In every challenge, we find our song.
The labor's dance, a sweet delight,
In echoes of joy, we find our light.

Serenade of the Heart

Underneath the stars we lay,
In silent whispers, night turns to day.
The moonlight dances, sweet and bright,
A serenade of dreams takes flight.

With every breath, your presence near,
A melody, the heart can hear.
Softly swaying, souls entwined,
In this symphony, love defined.

As warmth envelops, time stands still,
In every glance, a sweet thrill.
The notes of passion softly blend,
In the serenade, we transcend.

With tender words, we share our truth,
In every sigh, the spark of youth.
Together we compose our tune,
A serenade beneath the moon.

The Language of Passion

In every glance, a tale unfolds,
The language of passion, bold and gold.
A touch, a whisper, hearts collide,
In depths of feeling, we confide.

Words unspoken, yet we know,
The silent bond, it starts to grow.
With every heartbeat, we ignite,
A dance of souls, pure delight.

Through fiery storms and gentle skies,
The language of passion never lies.
In tender moments, love takes flight,
Two souls ablaze in the night.

Together we weave a tapestry bright,
Of dreams and hopes, merging light.
In every heartbeat, we create art,
The language of passion fills the heart.

Heartbeats in Rhythm

In the quiet moments, we align,
Two heartbeats echo, yours and mine.
With every pulse, a story told,
In love's embrace, forever bold.

Through valleys deep and mountains high,
Our rhythms dance, beneath the sky.
With every step, we find our way,
In perfect sync, we choose to stay.

The world may change, but we remain,
In heartbeats' rhythm, love's sweet refrain.
Together we move, with grace and style,
In unity's warmth, we walk each mile.

In echoes soft, our bond resounds,
In every heartbeat, love surrounds.
Together as one, we share this bliss,
In heartbeats' rhythm, eternal kiss.

Journey of the Heart

In the quiet moments of reflection,
We wander through the shadows of our fears.
With every step, a new direction,
The heart unfolds, dispelling tears.

Mountains rise and valleys beckon,
Each path we take, a choice to make.
The way is long, but we will reckon,
With love that holds through every quake.

Stars above guide our intentions,
In the night, they shimmer and glow.
With each heartbeat, deeper connections,
With every sigh, our spirits flow.

So we journey on, no need to part,
For every lesson shapes our soul.
Together we will chart the chart,
This journey of the heart, our goal.

Cultivating Bliss

In gardens where the sun does smile,
We plant our seeds of joy and grace.
With gentle hands, we span each mile,
Contentment grows in every space.

Each drop of rain, a sweet caress,
Nourishing the dreams we sow.
With open hearts, we find excess,
In moments shared, our spirits grow.

The fragrance of the blooming flower,
Reminds us of the love we spread.
With every hour, a rising power,
In blissful thoughts, our fears are shed.

So let us tend this fertile land,
Where happiness and hope entwine.
In unity, we make our stand,
Cultivating bliss, divine.

The Signature of Authenticity

Beneath the masks, we find the truth,
A tapestry of years and scars.
With every story, we reclaim our youth,
Each word a glimpse of who we are.

To be authentic is the key,
In every laugh, in every tear.
When we embrace our history,
We shed the doubts, we cast out fear.

The strength we find in vulnerability,
A bond unspoken, pure and real.
With open hearts, we rewrite destiny,
In every moment, learn to feel.

So let us hold our truth up high,
For in the light, we come alive.
The signature of who we are will fly,
Authenticity, our greatest drive.

Heartfelt Odyssey

Through the valleys low and the peaks so high,
We traverse landscapes of the soul.
With every heartbeat, we can try,
To seek the journey that makes us whole.

The whispers of the winds will guide,
As we navigate the storms of fate.
In every shadow, love will bide,
Empowering us to open the gate.

With every step, a story unfolds,
In laughter and tears, we find our way.
The warmth of hearts, the tales retold,
In this odyssey, we choose to stay.

So let's embark, hand in hand,
With faith as our compass, hope as our light.
For in this journey, together we stand,
A heartfelt odyssey, pure delight.

The Treasure of Devotion

Through trials and storms we stand strong,
A bond so pure, it can't be wrong.
In whispered thoughts, our hearts align,
Together we shine, like stars that entwine.

With every breath, our love will grow,
A river's flow, a sacred glow.
Hands intertwined, we face the dawn,
In the dance of life, we carry on.

Through darkest nights and brightest days,
Devotion lights our winding ways.
In laughter shared and tears released,\nIn this treasure, we
find our peace.

So cherish the moments, both big and small,
In the tapestry of love, we find it all.
For in devotion's gentle embrace,
We uncover life's truest grace.

Capturing Joy

In the flutter of wings, joy does rise,
In the laughter of children, the sunlit skies.
It dances in raindrops, sparking delight,
A fleeting moment that feels so right.

Chasing the echoes of soft, sweet song,
In the warmth of a hug, where hearts belong.
Bright blooms of spring bring sweet surprise,
In every new dawn, our spirits reprise.

Through simple pleasures, joy we find,
In shared stories that bind us kind.
In fleeting glimpses of everyday grace,
In every smile, joy finds its place.

So seize the moments, let laughter flow,
In the cradle of time, let happiness grow.
For capturing joy is an art we make,
With every heartbeat, we create the wake.

Pathways of Inspiration

Through winding roads where dreams reside,
In every twist, hope is our guide.
With brush and pen, we carve our fate,
Inspire the world, don't hesitate.

In gardens lush, where ideas bloom,
With every thought, dispel the gloom.
From whispered winds, we gather strength,
Creating beauty at every length.

With eyes wide open, we wander far,
In the deep, dark night, we'll find our star.
For every step we bravely take,
A new horizon, a path we make.

So walk the trails where passions glow,
Through valleys deep and peaks of snow.
Inspiration's light will never fade,
In every heartbeat, dreams are made.

The Pulse of Possibility

In the heartbeat of dreams, we find our way,
Each pulse a promise of a brighter day.
With hope unbound, the future calls,
In every challenge, opportunity sprawls.

As shadows cast doubts upon the ground,
Within our courage, strength is found.
With open hearts, we face the skies,
In the pulse of possibility, our spirit flies.

Through every setback, we rise anew,
In every failure, there's something true.
With passion as fuel, we reach for more,
In the pulse of our dreams, we explore.

Embrace the journey, let visions soar,
For each heartbeat opens a new door.
In the rhythm of life, let's dance and sing,
For from the pulse of possibility, our hopes take wing.

The Alchemy of Desire

In shadows deep, we find our dream,
A flicker soft, a gentle beam.
The heart ignites, a burning fire,
Through whispered hopes, we build desire.

With every breath, the pulse ignites,
In quiet nights, we chase new heights.
A potion mixed of trust and light,
Together we shall take our flight.

The world may spin, but we stand still,
In timeless moments, hearts fulfill.
A tapestry of souls entwined,
In every glance, pure love defined.

Through trials fierce, our passion grows,
Like rivers wide, our essence flows.
Together we embrace the fire,
In every spark, we find desire.

Radiant Redistributions

As dawn unfolds, the colors blend,
A canvas bright where dreams ascend.
The world awakes in vibrant hues,
Each brushstroke tells of hopes renewed.

Hands outstretched, we share the light,
Transforming shadows into bright.
With every gift, the heart expands,
In radiant love, we take our stands.

The sun descends, a golden glow,
With whispers soft of tales we sew.
In every line, a story gleams,
Reshaping lives, igniting dreams.

Through laughter shared, we lift the veil,
In every challenge, we prevail.
Together we weave the fabric true,
In unity's grace, the world is new.

The Joy in Artistry

Beneath the strokes, the spirit flows,
A dance of color, joy bestows.
With every note, creation sings,
In symphony, our heart takes wings.

From clay to paint, the visions bloom,
In crafted space, we find our room.
Fingers trace the dreams we hold,
In each design, our stories told.

The laughter greets the time we share,
In every piece, a breath of air.
Through joyous steps, our hearts align,
In artistry, our souls entwine.

When shadows fall, we rise with grace,
Creating light in every space.
Together, we embrace the art,
In joy we forge, never to part.

Embracing Your Craft

In quiet corners, passion brews,
With tools in hand, we shape our muse.
Each chisel strike, each careful line,
In dedication, our dreams combine.

The heartbeat echoes, firm and strong,
A melody of righting wrong.
With every flaw, a lesson found,
In perseverance, we are bound.

As seasons change, our skills refine,
Through trials faced, our spirits shine.
In every art, the heart reveals,
A testament to how it feels.

So take the leap, embrace your fate,
In every step, create, create.
The world awaits your vibrant spark,
In loving craft, ignite the dark.

Illuminated Paths of Passion

In moonlit glow, we wander far,
Each step a dance, each breath a star.
With hearts ablaze, we chase the night,
Igniting dreams, a radiant flight.

Through whispers soft, the secrets tease,
Our souls entwined, the gentle breeze.
In every glance, a spark is found,
Together lost, yet tightly bound.

Beneath the skies, our laughter weaves,
A tapestry of bold believes.
In twilight's hush, we carve our fate,
With passion's fire, we navigate.

So hand in hand, let shadows fade,
As paths of light our choices made.
With every heartbeat, courage grows,
In love's embrace, our garden glows.

Threads of Fulfillment

From dawn's first light, we weave our dreams,
With golden threads, life softly gleams.
Each promise holds a shimmer rare,
As hopes entwine, with tender care.

Through trials faced, our spirits rise,
Embracing truth in skies so wide.
In every stitch, our stories blend,
A quilt of life, on paths we mend.

In fleeting moments, joy is sewn,
With laughter's echo, seeds are thrown.
Each gentle thread, a bond we share,
A tapestry rich, beyond compare.

Together strong, we craft our fate,
With every choice, we celebrate.
In fullness found, we truly see,
The beauty held in unity.

Unveiling the Soul's Work

Within the depths of silent grace,
The whispers call, we find our place.
With open hearts, the veil we lift,
To see the light, a precious gift.

In shadows cast, the truth does gleam,
In quiet moments, we dare to dream.
Each piece revealed, a part of whole,
A journey deep into the soul.

With courage found, we face the day,
Embracing flaws, we find our way.
In every tear, a lesson learned,
Through love and loss, our spirits burned.

As layers peel, we come alive,
In unity, our hearts revive.
Through trials faced, the light we find,
Unveiling work of heart and mind.

Transformative Touch

A gentle nudge, a soothing hand,
Transforms our hearts, like grains of sand.
With every brush, the walls might fall,
A whisper shared, unites us all.

In tender moments, lives conjoin,
A spark ignites, an endless coin.
Each touch we share, a language pure,
In stillness found, we start to cure.

Through every heartbeat, warmth unfolds,
A tale of love that softly molds.
In fleeting glances, power flows,
A touch divine in joy bestows.

So let us cherish each connection,
Transformative, a bold direction.
For in each touch, we truly see,
The art of love, our legacy.

Passion's Palette

Brush in hand, the canvas waits,
Colors dance, as love creates.
Every stroke, a whisper sweet,
In this art, our hearts will meet.

Fires ignite with every hue,
Crimson dreams, and skies so blue.
A symphony of shades and light,
Painting souls through day and night.

With every color, stories bloom,
In passion's realm, we find our room.
A masterpiece both bold and clear,
In every heartbeat, love draws near.

The world a canvas vast and wide,
In love's embrace, we shall abide.
Together, we'll create our fate,
With passion's brush, we celebrate.

The Calling of the Heart

In silence deep, the heart will call,
Whispers soft, a gentle thrall.
It speaks of love, of dreams untold,
In every beat, a spark of gold.

Through valleys low and mountains high,
The heart won't falter, it won't lie.
It seeks the truth in every glance,
A dance of fate, a lover's chance.

The echoes loud, they guide our way,
In twilight's hush, we find our sway.
To heed the calling, brave and true,
To follow paths, both old and new.

With every pulse, our spirits soar,
A melody that speaks of more.
In tender moments, love will chart,
The sacred map within the heart.

Dreaming in Vivid Colors

Close your eyes, the world unfolds,
In dreams so bright, our story's told.
Through vibrant shades, we take our flight,
In canvas skies, we chase the light.

A splash of gold, a dash of blue,
In every dream, I glimpse you too.
Imagination's wings take flight,
We weave our visions, pure delight.

As shadows play, the colors sway,
In vibrant hues, we find our way.
Each dream a portal, bright and bold,
In vivid realms, our hearts unfold.

Awake or dreaming, side by side,
In every stroke, our souls abide.
Together painting, love we'll show,
Dreaming in colors, let it flow.

Vibrations of Authenticity

In every note, the truth will ring,
A song of life, authenticity we bring.
With voices clear, we'll raise our song,
In harmony, we all belong.

Through trials faced, we find our sound,
In victory's grace, our love is found.
No masks to wear, no need to hide,
In open hearts, we will abide.

Each vibration, a pulse of heart,
In every lyric, we play our part.
The beauty lies in being real,
In each connection, we shall feel.

Together we'll create a space,
Where all are free to find their place.
In authenticity's warm embrace,
Our spirits dance, in love and grace.

The Blissful Path

In morning light, the path unfolds,
With whispers soft and stories told.
Each step we take, a dance of grace,
Embracing peace in this sacred space.

The trees they sway with gentle flair,
Inviting us to breathe the air.
A symphony of nature's sound,
In every heartbeat, joy is found.

The river flows, a silver line,
Reflecting dreams that brightly shine.
The flowers bloom, a vibrant hue,
In every color, hope breaks through.

Together here, on this blissful way,
We savor life, come what may.
Hand in hand, through life we tread,
With love as compass, never dread.

Journey's Embrace

Through winding roads and skies so blue,
With every turn, we find something new.
The world unfolds in vivid dreams,
Guided by laughter, joy redeems.

In valleys deep, in mountains high,
We chase the stars, we learn to fly.
Every moment, a gift bestowed,
In every smile, our spirits glowed.

We gather stories, hand in hand,
Creating memories, our little band.
With open hearts, we face the strife,
In the embrace, we find true life.

So let us wander, let us roam,
In every step, we create a home.
Together here, our journey's art,
With love as our guide, we'll never part.

Serendipity of Skills

In quiet moments, talents wake,
With every stroke, new paths we make.
Crafting magic from simple tools,
In whispered dreams, we break the rules.

The hands that shape, the hearts that feel,
In every effort, we discover zeal.
From clay to song, the world's our stage,
In serendipity, we write our page.

Collaboration, a dance of grace,
Each voice a note in this vast space.
With countless skills combined as one,
In unity, our work's begun.

So let us grow, let passions soar,
In every challenge, we explore.
The every stumble, a chance to learn,
In the flame of creation, our spirits burn.

Crafting Joyful Moments

With every sunrise, a chance to play,
In simple joys, we find our way.
A shared laugh, a tender glance,
In these small moments, our hearts dance.

The art of living, a joyful call,
In family gatherings, we stand tall.
With every hug, our spirits lift,
In every gift, life's precious gift.

With stories woven, near and far,
Each memory shines, like a guiding star.
In the fabric of time, we stitch and weave,
Crafting joy in every eve.

So let's embrace each fleeting hour,
In laughter's bloom, we'll find our power.
Creating moments, rich and sweet,
With love as the rhythm, our hearts beat.

The Horizon of Serenity

Beyond the waves where silence dwells,
The sky paints dreams with pastel swells.
Gentle whispers in the breeze,
A symphony of rustling leaves.

Soft sunlight bathes the tranquil shore,
As seabirds call, forevermore.
In this space, the soul finds peace,
A moment's pause, a sweet release.

Clouds drift lazily, thoughts take flight,
Where the day fades into night.
Colors blend in a brilliant hue,
Every glance unveils something new.

At the horizon, time slows down,
In every echo, joy is found.
Here serenity's embrace is wide,
A canvas where the heart can glide.

Creation's Heartbeat

In the stillness, a spark ignites,
A dance of shadows, a chorus of lights.
Crafted whispers shape the air,
Each breath a tapestry, bold and rare.

From chaos, beauty takes its form,
In swirling colors, the universe warms.
Every particle sings a note,
As time and space weave dreams afloat.

With gentle hands, the cosmos spins,
A dance of beginnings, where life begins.
In silent rhythm, a heartbeat thrums,
In every moment, creation hums.

Energies join, a vibrant flow,
Through every valley, over every toe.
Nature's heartbeat, strong and fine,
In this grand art, the stars align.

The Serenade of Craft

In the workshop's glow, hands come alive,
Each crafted piece, a dream to thrive.
With patience, love, and gentle care,
Artisan's touch in the evening air.

Wood and stone, clay and thread,
Stories spoken, words unsaid.
The wheel spins slowly, a song unfolds,
In every grain, a tale retold.

Sculpted visions rise from earth,
A testament to skill and worth.
With every strike, the metal sings,
A melody of life's bright wings.

In harmony, the craftsman stands,
Creating wonder with skilled hands.
The serenade of craft, a delight,
A dance of passion, pure and bright.

Harvesting the Essence

In fields of golden grain, we roam,
Collecting dreams that lead us home.
Each ear of corn, each vine's embrace,
Holds stories of a sacred place.

Beneath the sun, the fruits await,
Nature's bounty, a joyful fate.
Harvesting laughter, joy, and tears,
Collecting colors from passing years.

The fragrance of earth fills the air,
Reminding us of love and care.
With every season, life renews,
In the essence of the morning dew.

Gather the moments, let them blend,
In this tapestry, we transcend.
Harvesting whispers, dreams in flight,
In every heartbeat, pure delight.

Pursuit of the Soul

In the quiet depths we seek,
Whispers of a truth unique.
Through the shadows, light we chase,
Journeying to a sacred place.

Every heartbeat sings a song,
Guiding us where we belong.
With each step, the path unfolds,
Stories waiting to be told.

Mountains rise, and valleys call,
In pursuit, we rise, we fall.
Yet with courage, we press on,
Seeking dawn, where dreams are drawn.

In the end, the soul awakes,
In the light, the heart partakes.
Freedom found, we've paid the toll,
In the journey, we find the soul.

An Echo of Exuberance

Laughter dances in the air,
Joy, a lightness everywhere.
Like the sun, it warms the heart,
In this moment, we take part.

Colors burst in every sound,
In this chaos, peace is found.
Every smile, a gift we share,
Rippling joy, beyond compare.

Time stands still, we feel alive,
In this spirit, we all thrive.
Let it echo through the night,
Spreading love, a pure delight.

Cherish every fleeting hour,
In exuberance, we find power.
Together, let our spirits rise,
An echo that never dies.

Embrace the Calling

Whispers beckon from within,
A voice that stirs, it's time to begin.
Hearts aligned with purpose clear,
Embrace the path, let go of fear.

Step by step, the road unfolds,
Every moment, alive with gold.
Chasing dreams, we find our way,
In the light of a brand-new day.

With open arms, we greet the skies,
Facing challenges, we shall rise.
In the calling, we find our truth,
A flame ignited in the youth.

Let it guide us through the night,
With every heartbeat, feel the light.
Embrace the calling, hearts in sync,
Together, on this edge, we think.

Elevation Through Dedication

Brick by brick, we build our dream,
With hard work, nothing's as it seems.
Dedication, a steadfast guide,
Through the storms, we shall abide.

Every challenge, a chance to grow,
In the trials, our strength will show.
Climbing high, we reach for stars,
In this journey, we'll heal the scars.

With passion fierce, we light the way,
Each small victory, a brand-new day.
Through sweat and tears, we find our grace,
Elevation's worth the chase.

In unity, we rise as one,
Together, brighter than the sun.
Through dedication, dreams take flight,
In the darkest hours, we find our light.

Dreams Woven in Diligence

In quiet moments, visions glow,
Where hope and labor intertwine.
Each step a stitch, in softest flow,
A tapestry of dreams divine.

With steady hands, we shape the light,
Through trials faced, our spirits rise.
Patience sown, we claim our fight,
In fields of effort, wisdom lies.

Each dawn we wake, with purpose clear,
Chasing shadows, casting doubt.
With every heartbeat, let us steer,
Towards horizons, wide and stout.

For dreams are born from seeds we sow,
In gardens rich, of time and care.
Through diligence, together grow,
A harvest bright, beyond compare.

Radiance of True Pursuit

Chasing stars in twilight's glow,
With every step, our spirits soar.
A journey full of highs and lows,
With every loss, we yearn for more.

In passion's fire, we find our way,
Through shadows deep and valleys wide.
With courage bright, we choose to stay,
In the heart of dreams, we bide.

The road may twist, the path may weave,
Yet purpose leads us, strong and true.
In every breath, we dare believe,
That light will pierce the heavy blue.

Through struggle's lens, we see the grace,
Of every moment, hard-fought gain.
In true pursuit, we find our place,
United in our joy and pain.

The Melody of Meaning

Soft whispers drift on evening breeze,
A tune that speaks of joy and strife.
In harmony, the heart finds ease,
A song that echoes through our life.

With every note, a story told,
Of dreams pursued and passions found.
In sweet refrain, our spirits bold,
Resonate with love profound.

The cadence flows with ebb and tide,
In rhythms deep, we dance along.
In every leap, in all we bide,
We find a strength within the song.

Together we'll compose our fate,
With each crescendo, rising high.
In every heartbeat, celebrate,
The melody of life's supply.

Harvesting Happiness

In sunny fields where laughter stays,
We plant the seeds of joy and cheer.
With tender care, through all the days,
We nurture dreams that bloom sincere.

The golden sun, it warms our toil,
As we till earth with hands and hearts.
In every row, rich friendship's soil,
A bounty grows, where love imparts.

When autumn calls, we gather close,
The fruits of kindness, sweet and bright.
In every smile, our hearts propose,
A harvest filled with pure delight.

So let us share, this simple truth,
In every moment, joy we find.
Through gratitude, and vibrant youth,
We cultivate a life entwined.

Manifesting Joy

In the garden of bright dreams,
Hope blossoms like the sun.
Whispers of laughter flow,
Embracing everyone.

With every step we take,
Gratitude lights the way.
Moments dance like fireflies,
Transforming night to day.

In the rhythm of our hearts,
Joy blooms without a care.
Infinite as the stars,
A treasure we all share.

Together we will rise,
Hand in hand, we'll explore.
In the light of our spirits,
Joy is forever more.

The Genius of Grit

With each challenge we embrace,
Strength awakens deep inside.
Resilience plants its roots,
In the storm, we will abide.

Like mountains in the mist,
We stand tall, unyielding.
Every stumble teaches us,
In our dream, we are wielding.

The fire within us burns bright,
Grit whispers through the night.
With courage as our guide,
We will always find the light.

In the face of doubt and fear,
We hold steadfast with pride.
For in the genius of grit,
True victories reside.

Heartfelt Endeavors

In the quiet of the night,
Dreams gather like the dew.
Every heartbeat echoes love,
In endeavors, pure and true.

With each stroke of our hands,
We paint the world anew.
Kindness flows like water,
In every act we do.

Chasing visions close at heart,
Together, we unite.
The strength of our connections,
Brings darkness into light.

In the dance of our intent,
We rise above the fray.
Heartfelt endeavors lead us,
To a brighter day.

Celebration of the Spirit

In the symphony of life,
We dance to every beat.
Souls entwined in harmony,
Moments bittersweet.

With laughter and with love,
We gather close and near.
Every story shared,
Brings warmth, and keeps us clear.

In the essence of our dreams,
Hope takes flight, a dove.
Celebration of the spirit,
Wrapped in joy, in love.

Together we transcend,
As shadows fade away.
In this canvas of our hearts,
We create a brighter day.